# BIKE RALLIES

## MOTORCYCLE MANIA

## David and Patricia Armentrout

Rourke

**Publishing LLC**
Vero Beach, Florida 32964

www.rourkepublishing.com

PHOTO CREDITS: Cover ©Matej Krajcovic; title page and pp. 4, 8, 10, 11, 14, 16, 18, 19 © John L Richbourg; pp. 5 © Douglas Litchfield; pp. 6 ©Dranzi; pp. 7 © Sgt. Clinton Firstbrook/USMC; pp. 9, 20, 21 ©Tracey Stearns; pp. 12 © Suzuki; pp. 13 ©Anson Hung; pp. 15 © Noel Clark; pp. 17 ©Honda; pp. 22 ©Maj. Mark T. Bodde/USMC.

Title page: *A couple cruises the strip at Daytona Beach.*

Editor: Robert Stengard-Olliges

Cover design by Nicola Stratford


**Library of Congress Cataloging-in-Publication Data**

Armentrout, David, 1962-
 Bike rallies / David and Patricia Armentrout.
     p. cm. -- (Motorcycle mania II)
 ISBN-13: 978-1-60044-586-6
 1. Motorcycles--United States--Juvenile literature. 2. Motorcycling--United States--Juvenile literature. 3. Motorcyclists--United States--Social life and customs. I. Armentrout, Patricia, 1960- II. Title.
 TL440.15.A756 2008
 796.7--dc22
                                    2007016374

**Printed in the USA**

CG/CG

Rourke Publishing

www.rourkepublishing.com – rourke@rourkepublishing.com
Post Office Box 3328, Vero Beach, FL 32964

# TABLE OF CONTENTS

# MOTORCYCLE RALLY

Imagine you're enjoying a warm, sunny day, when you begin to hear a low rumble of thunder off in the distance. You quickly realize it's not an approaching storm; it's a **convoy** of motorcycles heading in your direction—a sea of black leather and chrome.

There is one thing that attracts hundreds of bikers out on the road at the same time—a motorcycle rally.

*Motorcycle rallies are part of the motorcycle culture.*

*Rallies attract motorcycle riders from all around the country.*

# POPULAR ATTRACTIONS

A motorcycle rally is a gathering of motorcycle **enthusiasts.** Motorcycle clubs, bike builders, and racing associations sponsor rallies.

Bike rallies attract a **diverse** group and are growing in popularity. Rallies can be large or small, one time get togethers, or yearly events.

*Bikers gather for a rally parade.*

*Can you find the motorcycle in this picture?*

The American Motorcyclist Association (AMA), founded in 1924, protects and promotes the interests of motorcycle enthusiasts.

# MOTORCYCLE CULTURE

Motorcycle riders can feel out of place on the road because cars and trucks surround them. Joining a motorcycle club helps them feel like part of a community. Club members share common interests, like racing or off road riding. Participating in events, such as a motorcycle ride or rally, helps bikers stay connected to motorcycle culture, too.

Bike builders attend rallies to show off their custom motorcycles.

*Towns like Surgis, South Dakota support the biker community and welcome bikers every year to their rally.*

# MEET AND GREET

Rallies are vacations for many bikers. Cyclists begin weeks ahead—checking the oil, tires, battery, tightening loose bolts—preparing their motorcycles for a road trip.

Traveling is often an adventure, but the destination is what the trip is all about. Rallies are an opportunity for bikers to hook up with old friends, and to meet new ones.

*Rally goers pack the lot before the start of a custom bike show.*

*Bikers take pride in their machines.*

Rally organizers host plenty of events that keep bikers and non-bikers busy and entertained. Favorites include classic motorcycle rides and vintage motorcycle displays. There are also tattoo contests, arm wrestling competitions, and concerts. But the motorcycle competitions are the most exciting events. Huge crowds gather to watch motocross, hillclimb, superbike, and drag races.

*Motocross racing is a popular rally event.*

*Freestyle motocross riders entertain the crowd.*

When bikers get together they talk shop with others who share their passion. That's why some rallies are geared toward riders who are dedicated to certain motorcycle brands. The Honda Riders Club is a major sponsor of the Honda Hoot, a rally held in Tennessee. The Harley Owners Group (HOG) also sponsors numerous events and rallies throughout the year.

*New custom motorcycles attract attention at a bike show.*

*Loyal Harley-Davidson owners gather for a club event.*

# DAYTONA BEACH

Daytona Beach, Florida hosts one of the best-known bike rallies in the U.S. The first rally was in 1937. The main attraction was the Daytona 200 motorcycle race. It took place on a 3.2 mile (5.15 km) **circuit** that started on the beach, crossed over to a paved course, and then back to hard-packed sand. The 200-mile (322 km) race moved to the Daytona International Speedway in 1961.

*Hundreds of thousands of bikers head for Daytona Beach every March to attend the famous rally.*

The Daytona 200 was nicknamed the *Handlebar Derby* back in the 1930s.

*Honda rider Miguel Duhamel tests his bike prior to the Daytona 200 superbike race.*

The Daytona Beach Bike Week now takes place over a ten-day period in early March. The event attracts hundreds of thousands of people to the area. Bikers enjoy custom bike shows, races, live entertainment, and plenty of food and drink. Attendees browse the vendor displays selling rally souvenirs and motorcycle **paraphernalia**.

*Some riders travel hundreds of miles to attend bike week in Daytona.*

*A stunt rider performs for the Dayton Beach crowd.*

19

# THE BLACK HILLS

Sturgis, South Dakota hosts a rally every August. The first rally in 1938 was actually a race with only nineteen riders. Today the event is so big it takes a special city department to organize and promote it. Hundreds of thousands of people flock to Sturgis, many for the motorcycle racing events. But cruising the beautiful Black Hills of South Dakota could be what attracts riders the most.

*The rumble of motorcycle engines fills the air in Sturgis every August.*

*Some rally riders like to be noticed.*

# REASONS TO RALLY

Organizations may sponsor rallies to raise money for charities. Some groups simply love to put on a great party. Many bikers attend rallies for the racing. Others go for the custom bike shows where they can meet famous bike builders or get a chance to win a custom ride.

There are so many reasons to rally, but all rallies have the same goal—bikers having fun sharing their passion for motorcycle riding.

*Bikers prepare for a ride collecting toys for the Toys for Tots charity.*

# GLOSSARY

**circuit** (SUR kit) — a route that starts and finishes in the same place

**convoy** (KON voy) — a group of vehicles traveling together for convenience or safety

**diverse** (duh VERSS) — varied or assorted

**enthusiasts** (in THOO zee ists) — people who have a keen or strong interest

**paraphernalia** (pair uh fuh NAIL ya) — equipment, gear, or accessories

# INDEX

## FURTHER READING

Schuette, Sarah L. *Harley-Davidson Motorcycles*. Capstone Press, 2006.
Doeden, Matt. *Motorcycles*. Capstone Press, 2006.
Seate, Mike. *Choppers*. MBI Publishing, 2006.

## WEBSITES TO VISIT

www.amadirectlink.com
www.msf-usa.org

## ABOUT THE AUTHORS

David and Patricia Armentrout specialize in writing nonfiction books for young readers. They have had several books published for primary school reading. The Armentrouts live in Cincinnati, Ohio, with their two children.